A SIX-WEEK BIBLE STUDY

GOD
AND
Money

Joe Plemon & Bob Lotich

Published by Rendren Publishing © 2016 Joe Plemon & Bob Lotich

ISBN 978-0-9898945-5-5

To order additional copies of this resource, write to SeedTime Customer Service: 625 Baker's Bridge Avenue Suite 105 Box 134 Franklin, TN 37067; email contact@seedtime.com; order online at SeedTime.com.

Printed in the United States of America

Meet the Authors

Joe Plemon

Joe Plemon has been a Christian Financial Coach since 2006 and has helped hundreds of individuals and families create workable plans to eliminate their debt and get control of their money.

Joe lives in Anna, Illinois. He and his wife Jan have four children and eleven grandchildren.

Bob Lotich

Bob Lotich used his passion for Biblical personal finance to launch his award-winning blog, SeedTime.com in 2007. His writing and advice have been featured in Men's Health Magazine, Real Simple Magazine, Yahoo Finance, Forbes, and many others.

Bob currently lives with his wife Linda and son Alden in Franklin, Tennessee.

CHAPTER
ONE

GOD OWNS IT ALL

Behold, to the LORD your God belong heaven and the heaven of heavens, the earth with all that is in it. Deuteronomy 10:14

1 | GOD OWNS IT ALL

The charging horseman spotted John Wesley, jerked back on the reins, then shouted, "Mr. Wesley! Mr. Wesley! Something horrible has happened. Your house has burned to the ground."

John Wesley stood still, looked down for a moment and then up to the messenger. "No. The Lord's house has burned to the ground. That is one less responsibility for me." [1]

Had Wesley, an 18th century Anglican evangelist, embarked on a minimalist lifestyle? Not at all. Had he lost touch with reality? Hardly. How could he be so calm? He was convinced that God owned everything— including his house.

"Just a minute," you may be thinking. "God owns everything? I've always assumed that my weekly church offering was God's and everything else was mine."

I get that, but the underlying issue is who owns the money before you write that church check. Most people consider every penny to be theirs until they give some of it to God, but possession does not equal ownership, and most people have this ownership thing upside down. Consider these verses:

- Behold, to the LORD your God belong heaven and the heaven of heavens, the earth with all that is in it. (Deuteronomy 10:14)

- For every beast of the forest is mine, the cattle on a thousand hills. I know all the birds of the hills, and all that moves in the field is mine. If I were hungry, I would not tell you, for the world and its fullness are mine. (Psalm 50:10–12)

- The earth is the LORD's and the fullness thereof, the world and those who dwell therein. (Psalm 24:1)

God's Property Managers

Even though everything belongs to God, He expects us to manage it. Jesus told of a landowner (see Matt. 25:14–28) who, before going on an extended trip, divided his property among his servants. When he returned, the owner interviewed each worker to learn how well he had managed his assigned portion. He rewarded those who had done well but punished the one who did nothing.

What does Jesus want us to learn from this parable?

- There is an owner who goes away and returns. God, of course, is that owner. He came to Earth as the man Jesus, He ascended to heaven, and He will one day return to Earth (Acts 1:9–11).

- Jesus expects us, His servants, to manage the assets of planet Earth the same way He would if He were here in person. I am reminded of the time—as Power of Attorney for my uncle—I was admonished to "act in good faith for the best interest of the principal, using due care, competence, and diligence."

- Each of us will be held accountable for how well we managed God's property.

- We will be judged on how we have made God's assets grow—or not.

Why Would God Put Sinful Humans in Charge of His Assets?

God's ways are not our ways. Net worth, rates of return, and annual dividends mean little to God because His most valued possessions are people, not portfolios. He requires our management so He can mold our character, and He uses money as the catalyst. Why?

- We are forced to prioritize between God and money. Luke 16:13 (NIV) states, "No one can serve two masters. For you will hate one and love the other; you will be devoted to one and despise the other. You cannot serve both God and money." Choosing between God and money is seldom a black and white issue. Should you buy a new car? Should you remodel your kitchen? Should you order lobster or a hamburger? God knows there are no "one size fits all" answers, meaning He expects us to wrestle day to day, sometimes moment to moment, with whether our money decisions honor him. But this wrestling is a good thing because, in so doing, we are practicing in real time the concepts Jesus taught two millennia ago. And this constant practice draws us incrementally closer to God.

- Money management exposes our deepest motives. The rich young ruler (Mark 10:17–25) left Jesus in sorrow because he clung to his wealth. But Zacchaeus, the tax collector, (Luke 19:1–10) demonstrated his salvation by giving away much of his fortune.

- Managing God's money is more than a robotic bookkeeping exercise. He expects us to know His mind, His heart, and His will so we can think His thoughts and feel His feelings. The good news is that God is always approachable through prayer and His Word. The better news is that the more time we spend with Him, the more He will change us to be like him. And the best news is that God delights in sharing Himself with His children.

- We are naturally selfish, but God changes our hearts as we manage His money. I (Joe) have pinched pennies all my life, but as I have managed God's money over the years, I have seen God change my tight fistedness to a love of giving. I still have far to go, but He continues to mold me. Isn't God amazing?

- It's easier to give stuff away when it belongs to someone else. If your boss told you to write a $1,000 company check to a civic organization, you wouldn't think twice. But writing a personal check…well, that's a different matter. Or is it? Not if it all belongs to God in the first place.

So why would God put sinful humans in charge of His assets? Because He is in the people business, not the money business.

Making It Work

You may be thinking, "All this talk about God owning everything sounds good in theory, but I've got such a tight grip on 'my stuff' that I'm not sure I can let go. Any suggestions?"

Sure. Loosening our grip is difficult because doing so forces us to probe the deeper issue of surrender, not simply our possessions but our hopes, our dreams—our very lives. This surrender will likely happen in increments and may need to be repeated time after time. Jan and I (Joe) gave our daughter to God when she was born, but twenty months later, as she was battling a life-threatening infection, we gave her to God again…this time at a much deeper level.

The key is to get started. These tips will help:

- If married, discuss this "surrender" with your spouse. Flush out the ramifications, and make sure you are on the same page. This is not some emotionally charged decision but a calm, calculated commitment.
- Tell God it all belongs to Him. Be specific: your house, your car, your 401k, your children, each other. Say it out loud or write—and sign—a transfer of ownership document.
- Take some actions to jumpstart this surrender and cement it into your psyche. For example, you could do one or more of the following:

- Start giving in earnest to your local church.
- Loan—or give—your car (God's car) to a single mother or needy family.
- Dedicate God's television/computer/cell phone to activities he would approve of.
- Give away your surplus "stuff" to someone.
- Give of your time by helping others.

Scary? Most likely. But it helps to remember that it already belongs to Him anyway, that He is your heavenly Father, that he loves you, and that He is cheering for you.

It also helps to know that giving is the pathway to a deep, abiding happiness—a concept we will explore in the next chapter.

---

(1) http://www.epm.org/resources/2003/Feb/25/steward-and-master/

Action Items

Read the Parable of the Talents
from Mathew 25:14–28

Do one of the tips recommended
in "Making It Work."

Commit all of your
possessions to God.

Discussion Questions

Before reading this chapter, how did you think of ownership? It's all mine? My spouse's and mine? Some mine and some God's? All God's?

Has this chapter changed those views? Explain.

What is problematic for you about believing God owns it all?

When you think of managing God's assets (Parable of the Talents), what is difficult for you? What is liberating?

How has God used money issues to help you grow as a Christian?

Do you tend to think of yourself more as a servant or as a son/daughter? Explain.

Reread the tips from "Making It Work." Which ones do you struggle with? Why? What additional tips would you recommend in order to further anchor God's ownership into your everyday practices?

CHAPTER
TWO

UNDERSTANDING
GIVING

Each one must give as he has decided
in his own heart, not reluctantly or
under compulsion, for God loves a
cheerful giver.
2 Corinthians 9:7

2 | GIVING

At age 59, entrepreneur Jerry Caven was ready to kick back. He was a successful restaurateur, rancher, farmer, and real estate investor, and now he was looking for a nice lakeside retirement home. But the Owner of everything had other plans for Jerry.

"God led us to put our money and time overseas," Jerry says. "It's been exciting. Before, we gave token amounts, but now we put substantial money into missions. We often go to India."

What brought about Caven's new passion for giving? "It was realizing God's ownership," he explains. "Once we understood we were giving God's money to do God's work, we discovered a peace and joy we never had back when we thought it was our money!"[1]

You may be thinking, "If I had that much money, I'd be a great giver too." Maybe so, but the real issue is not what you would do but what you're doing right now. You may be giving a lot or not so much. Either way, this chapter will help you give God's way and discover joy in the process.

And the Bible, as always, is our guide. Let's dig in.

What Is a Tithe, and Why Should You Care?

The dictionary definition of tithe is "one tenth of annual produce or earnings." Abraham paid tithes to Melchizedek (Gen. 14:20), and Jacob vowed to God "...of all you give me I will give a full tenth to you" (Gen. 28:22). Eventually, Mosaic law required a tithe, and ten percent became the giving standard for the Jewish people.

The subject of tithing is one of great volatility in the Christian world. Some say that tithing is no longer relevant because the New Testament doesn't teach it. Others insist that since the Old Testament standard was never revoked, tithing is still required today.

But all this bluster becomes empty noise when one considers that Christians in America give only 2.5 percent of their incomes on average. We need to do better. So without getting caught up in the debate, let's agree that those who aren't tithing (75 percent of the church) would do well to set their sights on ten percent, while those who are already tithing should strive to do better.

Percentage Giving... Good or Not So Good?

Whatever you are currently giving, whether you realize it or not, is a percentage of your income. Should you use that percentage as a giving benchmark, or should you give whatever you can afford? Or maybe some of both?

Reasons Why Percentage Giving Can Be a Good Thing:

- Peace of mind. Giving a set percentage resolves the decision and ensures consistency.

- Percentage giving automatically ratchets your giving upward when you get pay raises. The reverse could also apply however; you would automatically give less (without feeling guilty) if your income decreases.

- The wealthy would give according to their incomes. Studies indicate that high earners give a smaller percentage than those with lower incomes.[3] Percentage giving would ensure that the affluent contribute at least their share.

Some Downsides of Percentage Giving:

- Tithing can lead to self-righteousness when givers rely on that ten percent for right standing with God. Jesus called such givers hypocrites, for they neglected "the weightier matters of the law: justice and mercy and faithfulness" (Matt. 23:23).

- Our giving could be based on legalism instead of love.

- We could become complacent with giving a set percentage, even a tithe. Complacent givers miss out on the joys of sacrificial giving.

A balanced approach makes a lot of sense: using a percentage to track our progress while striving to give more. Hopefully, over time, our giving will grow to fifteen percent or twenty-five percent or fifty percent. I have a friend who gives the percentage that matches his age. Exciting…and challenging.

Whatever our technique, Jesus is our model. "For you know the grace of our Lord Jesus Christ, that though He was rich, yet for your sake He became poor, so that you by His poverty might become rich" (2 Corinthians 8:9).

Jesus gave sacrificially out of love. We should too.

Keeping Our Motives Pure

Jesus is more concerned about why we give than how much we give. When the religious big shots of His day made a show of their giving (they actually sounded trumpets), Jesus assured these "hypocrites" that they would have "no reward from your Father in heaven" (Matthew 6:1 NIV).

What does God expect? 2 Corinthians 9:7 is a great guide: "Each one must give as he has decided in his own heart, not reluctantly or under compulsion, for God loves a cheerful giver." From this verse, we learn that giving should be 1) premeditated, 2) not out of duty, 3) not because someone is pressuring us, and 4) cheerful.

We should give consistently and consider it to be an act of worship. Paul admonished the church in Corinth to set aside their gifts on the first day of the week (1 Corinthians 16:2). Why the first day of the week? Because that day was the day of worship, meaning Paul expected the Corinthians to incorporate giving into their worship. The act of giving today should not be a commercial break in our church services but an integral part of our worship experience.

Scripture is clear that giving is much more than taking up a collection. God expects our giving to be something special between Him and us. He is displeased when we do it for show but loves it when we give cheerfully and consistently, in an attitude of reverence and worship.

Some Great Givers

We share these stories of great givers, not to draw attention to the individuals named but to inspire you to consider how you can do better.

- The widow, who gave her only penny (Mark 12:41–45)

Jesus sat watching people give offerings. Some gave large sums, but Jesus declared that this widow, who only gave a penny, had made the greatest contribution of all. Why? Because while others gave of their abundance, she gave everything she had.

Some Great Givers

- John Wesley, who capped his standard of living.

When Wesley (1703–1791) was a young man, his conscience was pricked because after spending all his money on himself, he was unable to purchase a coat to protect his chambermaid from the bitter cold. He vowed to maintain the same standard of living so that as his income would increase, he would have more to give. The first year, he lived on twenty-eight pounds and gave two pounds. The next year, his salary doubled, so he lived on twenty-eight pounds and gave away thirty-two. Eventually, as an Oxford professor, his salary reached over 1,400 pounds, but he continued to live on twenty-eight so he could give away the rest.

Wesley, who had no family to support, continued this practice throughout his life. He was so diligent about giving that at his death, his estate amounted to only a few coins found in his pockets and dresser drawers. He had given everything else away.

- R.G. LeTourneau, who gave 90 percent of his income to the Lord's work

LeTourneau (1888–1969) was a Christian industrialist who dedicated his life to being a businessman for God. He was hugely successful, designing and developing his own line of earth-moving equipment. LeTourneau was the maker of nearly 300 inventions and had hundreds of patents in his lifetime. As his earnings grew, so did his generosity, to the point where he gave 90 percent of his income to the Lord's work. LeTourneau once quipped, "I shovel out the money, and God shovels it back—but God has a bigger shovel."

- God himself, who gave away His only son

  John 3:16 says it all: "For God so loved the world, that He gave His only Son, that whoever believes in Him should not perish but have eternal life."

How to Give More
When You Think You Can't

Perhaps you want to become a better giver, but you doubt you could make it happen. You're not alone; such doubts are normal. But if you're willing to take some simple, commonsense steps, those doubts will dissolve, and you'll soon be giving more than you ever thought possible.

These tips, while not exhaustive, will help. Remember… you can do this.

- Pray

  God wants to partner with you in your giving, so ask for His help. You may be astonished by how many new and creative ways He will enable you to give more, and more, and more.

- If you're married, have a money conference.

  Discuss your current giving. How are you doing, and how would you like to be doing? Make sure the two of you agree before making any changes. This is critical because neither of you can—or should—do this alone. We'll dig deeper in "Chapter Six: Money and Family."

- For example, you may be currently giving five percent of your income but would like to give more. A short-term goal would be to make some immediate sacrifices in order to start giving more now.

A long-term goal would be to bump your giving by one percent every year. Sound mundane? Perhaps, but stay on task, and in twenty years, you'll be giving twenty percent more than you are now.

Whatever goals you set, put them in writing. If you're married, both of you should sign the document. If single, sign two copies. Keep one, and give the other to a trusted friend; then ask this friend to keep you accountable.

Five Tips for Achieving Those Goals

1. Make a budget

Two-thirds of Americans don't live on a budget, so most of you need to prepare one. All of you need to put "Giving" as the top item on your spending, ahead of all other expenditures. Why? Because once you decide that "Giving" is a non-negotiable, you will force yourself to cut back on lower priority items such as cell phone plans, cable TV, and eating out. But there is some good news: Most people who begin to live on a budget discover money they never knew they had. Why? Because their previously unbudgeted money had been slipping through the cracks.

2. Avoid tax refunds

If you ordinarily get a tax refund, claim more exemptions on your W-4 form so your money will make its way to your paychecks instead of to the IRS. A $4,800 tax refund, for example, could become a $400 a month pay raise.

3. Utilize your bonus checks

Those of you who are paid weekly or bi-weekly could be letting some money slip through your fingers. How? Fifty-two checks a year (weekly) means there are four months every year when you get a "bonus" check (five checks instead of four). The same principle holds true for those paid bi-weekly—there are two months each year when you receive three checks instead of two. Mark those special months on your calendar, and create a plan for those bonus checks.

4. Consider investing less for retirement

I know…this sounds drastic, but Jesus touts the benefits. "Do not lay up for yourselves treasures on earth, where moth and rust destroy and where thieves break in and steal, but lay up for yourselves treasures in heaven, where neither moth nor rust destroys and where thieves do not break in and steal" (Matt. 6:19–20). All earthly investments involve risk, but treasures in heaven are risk free…and pay eternal dividends.

5. Cap your standard of living

Where you place that cap is between you and God, but one thing is certain: If you aren't intentional about capping your standard of living, you will drift toward bigger homes, nicer cars, and more extravagant vacations. We already talked about incrementally bumping your giving (perhaps every time you get a pay raise). Wouldn't it be great to honor God by giving Him a chunk of that pay raise while keeping your standard of living the same?

Dream Big

Research by psychologist Liz Dunn shows that people are happier when they spend more on others than on themselves—research which confirms what Jesus said thousands of years ago: "It is better to give than to receive" (Acts 20:35 NIV).

For most of the world, these words are a platitude, but for followers of Christ, they are marching orders. I hope this chapter challenges you to be a great giver. The good news is that God will partner with you every step of the way, meaning the better you manage His assets, the more He will give you to manage. (Remember the parable of the talents from chapter one?) Wouldn't it be amazing to someday give twenty percent or thirty percent or fifty percent...or more? Of course it would.

Go for it—dream big!

Giving draws us to the very heart of God, but we close this chapter with a reminder that He wants us to honor Him with all of His money, not just the portion we give away. Chapter three will help us to plan and save…God's way.

(1) http://www.epm.org/resources/2003/Feb/25/steward-and-master/

(2) http://www.relevantmagazine.com/god/church/what-would-happen-if-church-tithed

(3) http://www.foxbusiness.com/features/2013/04/24/poor-middle-class-and-rich-who-gives-and-who-doesnt.html

Action Items

Follow at least one of the tips
to increase your giving amount.

Discussion Questions

Do you think of giving in terms of how little you can give and still please God? What would it take to change your mindset to "How can I give more?"

Are you better at giving your time or your money? Explain.

Have you been systematically increasing your giving over the past several years? Do you plan to? What obstacles might you encounter?

What are your thoughts (both positive and not so positive) about capping your standard of living?

Do you consider giving to be an act of worship? Why or why not?

What is your attitude about giving? Do you give willingly? Cheerfully? Begrudgingly? What would it take for your giving to become a joy?

CHAPTER
THREE

PLANNING
AND SAVING

A good man leaves an
inheritance for his children's
children. Proverbs 13:22

3 | PLANNING AND SAVING

Jim Smith is sixty-six years old and recently retired. He has a paid for house, zero debt, and a $1.4 million nest egg. Throughout his working career, he earned an average salary.

Jim's twin brother Joe also earned an average salary throughout his own working career. Joe would love to retire, but he has no savings, tons of debt, and barely enough cash flow to pay his bills each month.

Jim and Joe represent much of the working class in America. Sadly, Jim is the exception and Joe is the rule. The average family debt in America, including mortgage, credit cards, and student loans, is over $200,000.[1] Furthermore, about half of Americans have saved nothing for retirement, and 29 percent of American households over age 55 have neither a retirement plan or a pension plan.[2]

What is the difference between the Jims and Joes? Jim had a plan. Joe didn't.

What's the Problem?

Why do so many people fail so miserably with their money? Many, if asked, would give you a shrug and a blank look. But there are reasons, and understanding the problem is the first step toward fixing it.

Some have always been surrounded by poor money managers. Their parents lived paycheck to paycheck, never saved, and were on a first name basis with their local cash loan officer. Their friends drove cars they couldn't afford, bought the latest everything on credit, and pestered colleagues for loans "just until payday." With no positive role models and plenty of negative peer pressure, many people meander through life without ever considering having a plan.

Others fall prey to instant gratification and easy credit. They see the TV ad, they research it on the Internet, they obsess over the car or furniture or clothing or tools, they justify "no interest for 48 months," they convince themselves it's a bargain, and they buy it. Then the next thing. Then the next thing again.

Many who reach their forties, fifties, or sixties abandon hope because they believe "It's too late for me."

Still others, perhaps those who struggle with midlife crisis, block the reality of old age from their minds and somehow convince themselves that planning for the future will make it happen.

Unless we die prematurely, that future will happen, and the truth is, whatever our reasons for not planning, we are nevertheless responsible to do so.

The time to start is today.

What Should You Be Saving For?

The reason to save money is to pay for a future need. Joseph (see Genesis 41) was able to foresee a famine in Egypt, so he recommended that Pharaoh save grain in order to be prepared. As a result, Egypt was able to bless many nations during those years of famine. Our future needs are probably not as dramatic, but the principle is the same. We should save now to fund future needs. Some examples of those needs are:

- Emergency fund. Your grandmother called it a "rainy day fund" because she knew that storms would come. Your water pump could go out or you could lose your job, but emergencies will happen, and not saving for them is foolish.

- Upcoming payments. You need to save for any payments (insurance, taxes, etc.) that are not paid monthly. Christmas, contrary to common belief, is never an excuse to spend money you don't have. Save up and be ready.

- Vacation. You should never schedule a vacation unless you can save the money ahead of time. Our family plans vacations a year out so we'll know how much to set aside each month to be ready.

- Automobile. You may believe that "everyone has car payments," but everyone doesn't, and you shouldn't either. If you're currently making those payments, keep doing so until the car is paid off, and then continue driving that car while making those payments to yourself. You'll soon be paying cash for your vehicles while always saving for the next one.

- Retirement. I do not define retirement as lack of activity, laziness, or pleasure seeking. We never retire from serving God, but most of us will retire from employment because of health limitations, job mandates, or other reasons. We should therefore plan for such a time so that when it comes, we will be prepared to serve God without burdening our families or society.

- An inheritance for our children and their children. Proverbs 13:22 tells us that "A good man leaves an inheritance for his children's children." While leaving an inheritance is nowhere on many people's financial radars, this admonition should not be discounted. Doing so is a selfless discipline that will not only pass a blessing to our heirs but implant the importance of saving in their minds. This inheritance should transcend dollars and cents, as we will see in chapter six.

Two Extremes of Saving

Saving too little is an invitation for trouble, but saving too much is likewise dangerous. The Bible speaks of both extremes, so let's seek the proper balance.

1. Saving too much.

Jesus told a parable (Luke 12:16–21) of a farmer whose barns were so full that a bumper crop created a storage dilemma. His solution? Tear down his barns and build bigger ones. This plan so pleased the farmer, and his wealth was so great, that he figured he would be able to "relax, eat, drink, and be merry" for many years.

But he was mistaken, for "God said to him, 'Fool! This night your soul is required of you, and the things you have prepared, whose will they be?'" (verse 20). Jesus concludes with these words in verse 21: "So is the one who lays up treasure for himself and is not rich toward God."

Why was this man considered a fool? We can start with the obvious: He was consumed with himself, as evidenced by nine first person pronouns in a three verse span. He was also short-sighted, making all his plans for this life and none for the life to come. And, of course, God was a non-factor in his life. This extreme saver thought himself quite clever, but he was a fool.

2. Saving too little.

Not saving enough is also foolish because funds won't be there when needed. Jesus told of a man who laid the foundation for a tower but couldn't complete it because he had failed to count the cost (Luke 14:28–30). All who saw his half-finished project mocked the man, saying, "This man began to build and was not able to finish" (verse 30).

For many, failure to save is a chronic problem, which can be ruinous, both to individuals and to families. Proverbs 6:6–11 challenges us to learn from the ant, who is a self-starter, consistently industrious, and needs no prodding from a "chief, officer, or ruler." The ant saved when he had opportunity so he would have food when he needed it. Verse 11 tells the sad outcome for those who lack the diligence of the ant: "Poverty will come upon you like a robber."

Finding the Proper Balance

Proverbs 30:8–9 was the prayer of a man who was seeking this very balance. "…give me neither poverty nor riches; feed me with the food that is needful for me, lest I be full and deny you and say, 'Who is the LORD?' or lest I be poor and steal and profane the name of my God."

The man recognized his own weaknesses, realized that either wealth or poverty could trigger them, and thus asked for neither. We should do the same, being ever mindful of our own weaknesses.

While wealth is a stumbling block for many, we should point out that some can handle wealth quite well. Paul explains how this is done in 1 Timothy 6:17–19: "As for the rich in this present age, charge them not to be haughty, nor to set their hopes on the uncertainty of riches, but on God, who richly provides us with everything to enjoy. They are to do good, to be rich in good works, to be generous and ready to share, thus storing up treasure for themselves as a good foundation and for the future, so they can take hold of that which is truly life."

Got it? God allows some of His children to have riches if their wealth doesn't go to their heads, if they trust God instead of their money, and if they are generous, doing good with what God gives them.

Making It Work

Knowing you should save and doing it are two different things. These tips will help.

- Think positively. You may be venturing into the unknown, but it is a good unknown. You have everything to gain and nothing to lose, so embrace the process.

- You must have a budget. We aren't talking about a bean counting exercise but an action plan that will change your life. I love Dave Ramsey's definition of a budget: "Telling your money what to do instead of wondering where it went." Your budget will reflect your priorities in life and guide you to keeping those priorities. Will it work perfectly the first month you try it? Probably not, but it will work better the second month and even better the

third month. This is a lifetime plan, so allow yourself time to make adjustments, and you will eventually develop a budget mindset. We will discuss budgeting further in chapter six.

- Make your savings automatic. I can't emphasize this enough. Why? So it will actually happen. You may have doubts about making ends meet once these savings deductions begin, but consider this: Most of you have lived with automatic income tax deductions for years. Do you get by? Of course. You simply adapt to whatever your take-home pay turns out to be. Automated savings work the same way, with one wonderful difference: The deducted funds go to you instead of to the IRS.

What sorts of savings should you have automated? Basically all. Some examples are:

Short-term savings

Have money you know you will need this year (property taxes, insurance payments, Christmas) automatically transferred into a "non-monthly payments" account.

Long-term savings

Are you building your emergency fund? Great. Have a set amount transferred every month into an Emergency Fund savings account.

Earmarked savings

Items such as car replacement and remodeling would be longer-term savings, while a vacation would normally be short term. Either way, each savings item should be earmarked and automated.

Retirement savings. If your employer offers a 401k or 403b plan, it is already automated. Isn't this easy? Sign up and take advantage. If you don't have a retirement plan at work, you should start an IRA, and then designate an amount to transfer into that IRA each month.

Remember: Keep it automatic, and it will always happen.

Would You Fire Yourself?

Imagine that you have been hired to oversee the construction of a million dollar building. The foundation has been poured, the walls are framed, and your boss asks you, "How are we doing on the budget?"

Now imagine that you have no clue. Would you keep your job? Probably not. But most families will manage over a million dollars of income in their lifetimes—money God expects them to manage wisely. If you had hired yourself to manage your money, would you fire yourself? Perhaps, but you should hire yourself back once you commit to managing God's money His way.

Chapter Three

I'm confident you can do this, but would the fringe benefits of less worry and more contentment provide some bonus incentives? I hope so. We will examine those benefits in chapter four.

(1) http://money.usnews.com/money/blogs/my-money/2014/07/01/5-things-keeping-americans-from-financial-freedom

(2) http://www.cnbc.com/2015/06/03/most-older-americans-fall-short-on-retirement-savings.html

Action Items

Read Genesis 41, the account of Joseph, Pharaoh, and the famine.

Start an automated savings in at least one of the suggested examples.

Discussion Questions

Do you (and your spouse, if married) live by a written budget? If not, why not? If you do, how do you make it work? What are your biggest challenges?

Do you tend to save too much (like the rich fool) or too little?

How are you doing at finding a healthy balance for your savings? What are some challenges you are facing while trying to find this balance?

Do you have targeted goals for your savings? How would these goals impact your motivation to save?

Do you automate your savings? How is it working? Which savings do you need to start automating?

If you have substantial wealth, do you handle it more like the rich farmer in Luke 12:16–20 or the rich man in 1 Timothy 6:17–19? How could you do better?

What have you learned in this chapter that will help you better honor God with your money management?

CHAPTER
FOUR

LEARNING CONTENTMENT

Not that I am speaking of being in need, for I have learned in whatever situation I am to be content. Philippians 4:11

4 | CONTENT-MENT

John D. Rockefeller, founder of Standard Oil, was a billionaire in the early twentieth century and is considered by many to be the richest man in modern history. A reporter once asked Rockefeller, "How much money is enough?"

His response? "Just a little bit more."

We may laugh, but many of us, regardless of our wealth, would say (or think) the very same thing.

How about you? Not sure? Try this exercise. Sit still and clear your mind of distractions. Now ask yourself, "Do I believe that my life would be better if I had just a little more money?"

How did you answer? And what did your answer tell you about yourself?

Money and Happiness

Richard Easterlin, Professor of Economics at the University of Southern California, has spent much of his career studying the correlation between money and happiness. The results may surprise you.

"Consider," Easterlin reports, "Americans born in the 1940s. Between the years 1972 and 2000, as their average age increased from about 26 to 54 years, their average income per person—adjusted for the change in the price of goods and services—more than doubled, increasing by 116 percent. Yet, their reported happiness in the year 2000 was no different from that 28 years earlier. They had a lot more money and a considerably higher standard of living at the later date, but this did not make them feel any happier."[1]

You may be thinking, "I didn't need a fancy research project to tell me the obvious. Everyone knows that more money doesn't produce more happiness."

Really? I refer you to the self-test you took a few minutes ago. Again…how did you answer? It seems that we acknowledge the disconnect between money and happiness, but we struggle to believe it applies to us.

Our challenge, therefore, is to develop a contentment—a God contentment—that will remain constant regardless of how much money we have—or don't have.

Our source, once again, is the Bible.

God's Definition
of Contentment

Paul wrote these words to Timothy long before Easterlin performed his studies: "Now there is great gain in godliness with contentment, for we brought nothing into the world, and we cannot take anything out of the world. But if we have food and clothing, with these we will be content" (1 Timothy 6:6–8 ESVUK).

Paul's "contentment connection" isn't with money—it's with God. The two (contentment and godliness) are irrevocably intertwined, for godliness without contentment would be a self-righteous and unsettled faith, while contentment without godliness implies a watered down faith, lacking in God's truth. And, of course, neither godliness nor contentment are dependent upon our financial well-being.

Paul continues in this letter (vs. 9–10) to spell out the dangers in desiring riches. Doing so invites temptations, harmful desires, and evil. This pursuit causes some to wander from the faith and even to do great harm to themselves.

We can therefore conclude that God expects us to be both godly and content, regardless of our circumstances. And, in case we still think we need "just a little bit more," Paul warns that the pursuit of riches is detrimental to both contentment and godliness.

But Surely Not in My Circumstances

We sometimes read Scripture through stained glass filters, ascribing clear instruction to "those people in the Bible" while failing to apply those same instructions to ourselves. Therefore, at the risk of redundancy, I cite another passage that states unequivocally that contentment is always possible, under any circumstance.

It is fitting that Paul writes these words (Phil. 4:11–13) from a prison cell: "Not that I am speaking of being in need, for I have learned in whatever situation I am to be content. I know how to be brought low, and I know how to abound. In any and every circumstance, I have learned the secret of facing plenty and hunger, abundance and need. I can do all things through Him who strengthens me."

If anyone could claim contentment "in any and every circumstance," it was Paul. In addition to his imprisonment, he had been given 39 lashes five times, beaten with rods three times, shipwrecked three times, and stoned once, and he was often without food or in cold and exposure. Furthermore, he faced constant stress because of his anxiety for all the churches. (see 2 Corinthians. 11:23–28)

Learning Contentment

Surely if Paul could be content in his circumstances, we can be content in ours. But how did he do it? And how can we do it? These tips will help:

- It takes time. We don't receive contentment from some magic elixir; we acquire it through the life experiences God gives us. Paul learned "in whatever situation to be content," so it's all right for us to give the process some time.

- True riches are crucial to contentment. What true riches am I talking about? The "great gain in godliness with contentment" that Paul wrote Timothy about. Godliness is a quality we receive—not achieve. Our role is to step back and allow God's Spirit to fill us and change us. He can and will do so, and we will become the recipients of godliness, a prerequisite and partner of contentment.

- Don't seek worldly riches. If "the love of money is the root of all kinds of evil" (which it is), then this misdirected love is the very antithesis of contentment. Stick with true riches.

- Appreciate what you have. Paul didn't own much, but he was content to have food and clothing. Do you have food and clothing? Tell God thank you. How about health, a job, a house, a car? Gratefulness, even about the smallest things—and sometimes for the smallest things—will help you learn contentment.

- Keep a perspective.

  Don't fall into the trap of comparing yourself and your stuff with friends, neighbors, family, and their stuff. Doing so breeds covetousness, not contentment. A better perspective is a global comparison. For example, if you earn $40,000 annually, you are ahead of 99.4 percent of the people in the world.[2] Like I said, be grateful.

God Comes to the Rescue

We have learned that money will never satisfy, and we have learned that the apostle Paul was able to be content while enduring extreme hardships. We have learned that this contentment is possible for us today, and we have learned some hints on how to bring it about.

But I wonder…have we been learning the *how to* of contentment without recognizing the *source* of contentment?

The dilemma is that contentment, much like happiness, can't be found by seeking it. But rest assured, it *can* be found, and this is the very best part.

God gives it to us.

How? By making and keeping a simple promise: "…be content with what you have, for He has said, 'I will never leave you nor forsake you'" (Heb. 13:5).

What more could we ask for? His unilateral promise, no strings attached, is to never leave us or forsake us. Is it any wonder that we should be content when we have the greatest treasure the world has ever known?

How could we *not* be content?

(1) http://www-bcf.usc.edu/~easterl/papers/Happiness.pdf

(2) http://www.globalrichlist.com/

Action Items

Write a list of 25 things
you are thankful for.

Discussion Questions

How did you answer the question "How much money is enough?"

....
....
....

Do you consider yourself content? Explain.

....
....
....

In your life, when have you been the most content?

....
....
....

What things do you worry about? Does worry help? What would it take for you to not worry?

....
....
....

Do you believe it is possible to be content no matter what your circumstances are? What would it take for you to experience this level of contentment?

....
....
....

Take time to review the section "Learning Contentment." Which of the hints were most helpful? What additional hints would you add?

....
....
....

The very last section tells of God coming to the rescue. Has He come to the rescue in your life? Explain.

....
....
....

CHAPTER
FIVE

THE TRUE COST OF DEBT

The rich rules over the poor, and the borrower is the slave of the lender. Proverbs 22:7

5 | DEBT

"You've come a long way, baby."

This Virginia Slims slogan from 1968 touted how far women must have come to have a cigarette designed especially for them, but the phrase itself has come a long way, eventually eclipsing the cigarette it once promoted.

Debt in America has likewise come a long way. People have, historically, sacrificed so they could avoid debt, but few people today think they can live without it. How did this happen?

At the beginning of the twentieth century, debt was commonly considered sinful or, at best, a character flaw. The 1910 Sears catalogue stated in bold letters, "Buying on credit is folly." JC (James Cash) Penney always paid cash, and the JC Penney stores never offered credit while their founder was alive. Henry Ford was resolute in not allowing his automobiles to be sold on installment plans, but he eventually acquiesced after his competitors began offering credit.

The biggest single factor in helping debt "come a long way" was the innovation of the credit card, beginning in 1946 with a "CHARG-IT" card. The Diners Club Card made its debut in 1949 and American Express in 1958, and these were soon followed by Visa, MasterCard, Discover, and others.

As the credit card industry grew, disdain for debt dropped. Owning a credit card, or the "right" credit card, became sophisticated—even chic—and, as one would expect, Americans amassed more and more debt. In 2015 the average credit card debt was $16,140. Other debts also escalated; the average mortgage debt was $155,361, and the average student loan debt was $31,946. [1]

As debt became more and more in vogue, guess what fell out of fashion? Savings, which plummeted from 11 percent of household income in 1982 to one percent in 2005. [2]

The True Cost of Debt

All this debt comes at a cost, most obviously the interest charges. A family that owes $10,000 on an eight percent car loan, owes $3,000 on a twelve percent credit card, has a $20,000 student loan at six percent, and has a $150,000 six percent mortgage may think, "We're only normal. Debt is a way of life." But this way of life is costing them $947 a month in interest—$454,560 over a forty-year period.

Shocking? Perhaps, but the cost of debt transcends interest payments. Money that is obligated to creditors each month is money that can't be used in other, more productive ways. For example, if that $947 per month could have been invested for those 40 years, it would have grown into a multi-million-dollar nest egg.   This is a lost opportunity and some mighty expensive debt!

The fact that many marriage breakups are directly linked to debt should surprise no one. After all, money problems are the number one cause of divorce in America, and debt is the number one cause of money problems.

Extravagant interest payments...lost opportunity costs...unprecedented divorce rates—all attributed to debt. It's enough to make you ill. Actually, it does. Numerous health issues, including chronic stress, depression, anxiety, heart conditions, diabetes, hair loss, excessive weight gain, and loss of libido, can all be linked to debt.

So here we are, a society that is so addicted to debt that we plug our ears, cover our eyes, and plow forward no matter the cost. Is there a cure? Let's see what the Bible has to say.

Is Debt a Sin?

Debt is never identified as sin in the Bible, but it *is* a form of slavery. Proverbs 22:7 tells us, "The rich rules over the poor, and the borrower is the slave of the lender." How is debt slavery? Because the one who loans the money owns a slice of the borrower—not only the payments, typically due for years into the future, but the time he must work to earn the money for those payments. Depressing? Of course. Slavery always is.

Whatever portion of your time and resources this slavery consumes is that much kingdom work being put on hold. It is no wonder that debt is always discouraged in Scripture.

Debt, by the way, is also scorned by the fiscal elite. Seventy-five percent of the Forbes 400 wealthiest people agree that "The number one key to building wealth is to get out of debt and stay out of debt."

What about Borrowing to Buy a House?

Borrowing to purchase a house is not to be viewed as a loophole for accumulating debt, but it can, with certain guidelines, be a good alternative to renting. Even then, the challenge is to be wise with God's money, borrowing as little as possible while planning to eliminate the debt as quickly as possible. These guidelines will help:

- Pay off all other debt first (including car loans, credit cards, and student loans).

- Build an emergency fund of six to twelve months' expenses before buying. Emergencies happen. The furnace could go out, or you could lose your job. Be prepared before signing a mortgage.

- Don't obligate more than 25 percent of your take-home pay for your house payment. It's one thing to own a home but quite another to let the home own you.

- Keep your repayment plan at 15 years or less. You will pay $63,514 in interest for a 15-year, five percent APR, $150,000 loan. The interest charges on the same loan, if spread over 30 years, are $139,883, meaning you "earn" a $76,369 bonus by opting for the 15-year plan.

- Consider a fixer upper. If you have the aptitude for remodeling, your sweat equity could pay off big time. All profits when you sell (up to $250,000 if single or $500,000 if married) is tax free when you have lived in your home for at least 24 months. Yes, we're talking about a lot of sacrifice, but if you buy, fix up, and sell a couple of times, you could own your home outright in only a few years. Note: Tax laws have a tendency to change, so be sure to double check.

What Does a Lifestyle of Debt Say About Us?

A person with a debt lifestyle charges everything, from his car to his quick meal. He owes money to credit card companies, furniture dealers, electronic stores, home improvement stores, and car dealers. He has lost track of how much debt he owes and has no plan to pay it off.

How would you describe a person who buys what he wants, when he wants, even if he doesn't have the money? Self-centered? Impatient? Short sighted? On the surface, this person may appear to be living a dream life, but what is happening beneath the surface? Even if he is making the payments, does the emptiness of it all nag at his subconscious? And if the debt load outweighs the income, then what? Anxiety? Health issues? Marital problems? Hopelessness?

The debt lifestyle is rooted in self and can only be overcome by the recognition that everything belongs to God (see chapter one). Then, and only then, can "self" be properly relegated to back burner status. Then, and only then, can the debtor be liberated from the slavery he is in. Then, and only then, can the believer in Christ become a disciple of Christ. (Mark 8:34)

Honoring God with a Debt-Free Lifestyle

We are not implying that those who live with debt cannot honor God, but they do so at a handicap because the interest paid on that debt—money that could otherwise go to kingdom work—is already obligated to creditors.

But God wants more than our money. He wants our hearts. It helps to look at the world through God's eyes and ask, "What is important to Him?" Doing so will allow God to change us so we will want to honor Him, not only with our money but with our lives.

How can married couples honor God? It starts with communication. Discuss how seeking God's plan together will change the dynamics of your marriage and your money. Dig deep. Listen to each other. Talk through habits and expenditures that, if purged, would free up funds to pay down debt.

You may be wondering if you should temporarily give less to God in order to pay off debt quicker. "After all," this reasoning would say, "if debt is such a negative thing, surely God would want me to use some of His money to get rid of it." The only problem is that Scripture does not give us license to pare back our giving to God.

Sure, getting out of debt could be expedited, but perhaps God knows that the process will be more meaningful if more sacrifice is required. Jesus put it this way: "But seek first the kingdom of God and His righteousness, and all these things will be added to you" (Matt. 6:33). Bottom line? Put God first, and everything else (including debt reduction) will take care of itself.

Tips for Dumping Debt

Ready to get rid of that debt? Great! For now, let's focus on all debt except your house. These tips will help:

- Quit borrowing money. It is impossible to pay off debt while creating more debt. Does this include credit cards? Yes, because every time you swipe one, you are borrowing money. If you can't break the habit, don't carry them with you. Proverbs 22:3 (NLT) could have been written just for credit card users: "A prudent person foresees danger and takes precautions. The simpleton goes blindly on and suffers the consequences."

- Set a time goal. Try for two years or less. Why? Because you will make greater sacrifices if you know it's for a limited time period. For example, you would need a little over $1,000 a month (depending on interest rates) to pay off $24,000 in two years. If your current payments are $500 a month, you'll need any combination of budget cuts and additional income for another $500. Sacrifice? Sure. Can you do it for two years? Of course.

- Sell stuff. It can be big or little, but it should always be with the goal of debt reduction. For example, if you sell a car you owe $20,000 on and buy a different one with a $5,000 loan, you would reduce your debt by $15,000. Give everything in your house a critical look, and sell it if you can. Learn your way around Craigslist, become a yard sale expert, or both.

- Take an extra job…or two. Yes, it will probably involve weekends, evenings, or both, but an extra job could bring in an extra $1,000 a month. Remember: It's only for two years.

- Use a debt snowball. A debt snowball works because of the power of focus. Start by listing all debts from smallest to largest, pay the minimum payment on everything except the smallest one, then focus on it with every penny you can find. Once it's gone, focus on the next smallest debt. Make sense? Every time you pay off a creditor, the amount you will be able to pay on the "new" smallest debt will grow…thus a debt snowball. To gain momentum, stick your list of debts on the refrigerator, and draw a huge red line through each one as you pay it off.

Congratulations! You have a plan, you're making it work, and you will soon be free from the bondage of debt. This will, of course, change your family forever, as we will explore in chapter six.

---

(1) https://www.nerdwallet.com/blog/credit-card-data/average-credit-card-debt-household/

(2) http://www.americanhistoryusa.com/give-me-liberty-or-give-me-debt-a-history-of-credit-cards/

(3) $457 per month, earning an eight percent annual return, will grow to $3.3 million in 40 years.

(4) https://www.daveramsey.com/index.cfm?event=askdave/&intContentItemId=117342

Action Items

List all of your debts from smallest
to largest.

Follow at least one of the tips for
dumping debt.

Discussion Questions

How has the way your parents handled money (and debt) affected you?

In what ways is debt like slavery to you?

Some people talk about "good debt." Do you consider any debt to be "good"?
Explain.

If you're married, how well do you and your spouse communicate about money?
About debt? Is one of you a spender and the other a saver? How can you learn
from each other?

If you're single, what advantages do you have over married couples for forming a
debt reduction plan? What are the disadvantages for a single person?

What are the main obstacles you see right now to becoming debt free? How are
you planning to overcome those obstacles?

CHAPTER
SIX

MONEY AND FAMILY

So they are no longer two but
one flesh. What therefore God
has joined together, let not man
separate. Matthew 19:6

6 | MONEY AND FAMILY

Gary and Candi were drowning in debt while their marriage was barely treading water. They knew something had to change, so they hired a financial coach and went to work.

A year later, they sent me a letter, which I quote with their permission: "We are happy to say that we are still together and that our marriage is stronger than ever. We won't lie; it has been a LONG year, and we have stumbled with staying on our budget more times than we can count."

Gary and Candi were excited about paying off $23,905 of debt that year, but they were more thrilled about how they had been able to keep up with their giving. "We never missed a pay period of tithing for the whole year! God has blessed us abundantly!"

These two had been transformed from a couple of frazzled individuals into a fired up team focused on paying off debt. In the process, they discovered, quite unexpectedly, that getting their money under control probably saved their marriage.

Is this connection between money and marriage an anomaly? Not at all. In fact, studies confirm what most of us already suspect: Money problems are marriage problems.

The Top Predictor of Divorce

Dr. Sonya Britt, program director of personal financial planning at Kansas State University, used data from more than 4,500 couples to assess exactly which issues cause a marriage to fail. "Arguments about money is by far the top predictor of divorce," said Dr. Britt. "It's not children, sex, in-laws, or anything else. It's money—for both men and women."

Wealth and poverty were irrelevant factors. "In the study, we controlled for income, debt, and net worth," Britt said. "Results revealed it didn't matter how much you made or how much you were worth. Arguments about money are the top predictor for divorce because it happens at all levels."

One reason money fights are so damaging is because they are more intense than any other kind of argument and therefore take longer to recover from. "Continued financial arguments decrease a couples' 'relationship satisfaction,'" Britt said.

But...This Study Is Good News

Good news? Yes, and here's why. If we know the top predictor of divorce, then we know the top issue to work on for a healthy marriage. And this news keeps getting better because once the husband and wife get on the same financial team, a peace will permeate throughout the family, creating an environment for teaching their children how to handle money. And these children will pass that knowledge on to their children. Good news indeed!

Marital Money Management–How Do We Do This?

Start by recognizing that you are already on the same team and that God is the glue.

"So they are no longer two but one flesh. What therefore God has joined together, let not man separate" (Matt. 19:6). When God made the two of you one flesh, He included your money—no matter who earned what or who brought what into the marriage. Affirm this union by looking each other in the eye and repeating, "God has joined us and our money together. None of our money is mine. It is all ours, and I pledge to honor God's plan by working with you to manage our money together." Got it? Great! Let's move on.

Embrace your differences.

Yes, you are one unit, but you are composed of two parts—often two very different parts. For example, one of you may be a saver, while the other is a spender. Or one may be more spontaneous and the other more regimented. Whatever those differences, embrace them. You both need what the other brought into the union. The late Larry Burkett, a prolific financial writer, said, "Opposites attract. If two people just alike get married, one of you is unnecessary."

Marital Money Management– How Do We Do This?

Establish your financial goals.

Start by individually writing out your goals. Include short-term (five years or less) and long-term goals (more than five years).

Compare the results, and discuss where you agree and disagree. Will this get testy? Perhaps, but that's good because you are actually communicating about money. This may be a good time to read 1 Corinthians 13:4–6 together: "Love is patient and kind; love does not envy or boast; it is not arrogant or rude. It does not insist on its own way; it is not irritable or resentful; it does not rejoice in wrongdoing, but rejoices in the truth."

At this point, you're flushing out the big picture issues, so don't feel that you need to work out every detail...yet. You may have already discussed the following, but, if not, do so now.

- Debt (see chapter five): How much debt is okay? How radical are you willing to be in order to get rid of your debt?

- Giving (see chapter two): How much should you give? Where? Local church? Elsewhere?

- Spending: How much is okay for one spouse to spend without checking first with the other? Don't forget Christmas spending.

- Retirement: When would either or both of you want to retire? What do you need to be doing now to make that happen?

Once you agree on your goals (or even if you agree to disagree for now in certain areas), move on to the next step.

Create a budget designed to help you meet your goals.

If one of you loves numbers and spreadsheets, great. Use that passion to create a preliminary budget. I say "preliminary" because it is going to change when you have your first budget meeting.

Budget meeting? Indeed. Once the preliminary budget is ready, put the kids to bed, turn the TV off, and meet. The one who prepared the budget should explain it to his/her spouse but (and this is critical) should not dominate or control the meeting—or even want to. After all, you two have already agreed on your goals, so allow the budget to be your friend in achieving those goals.

The other spouse also plays a critical role. He/she must listen, ask questions, understand how this plan works, and change at least one item. Why? Two reasons: to claim joint ownership of the budget and to let the numbers guru realize that this masterpiece can be modified.

Once you agree to the plan, try it for a month. Ideally, your kickoff should be at the beginning of a month so your numbers will coincide with a full month's billing cycle. Schedule ongoing budget meetings for the first of every month to discuss what didn't work and to make needed changes. These meetings are not negative; they are realistic. Most budgets take several months of fine tuning before they function as they should, so rather than despairing when it isn't perfect, plan ahead of time to fix it. A huge fringe benefit is that these monthly meetings (which should only last about fifteen minutes) are great opportunities to review and monitor your goals. Your momentum will build, and what may have begun as drudgery will eventually turn to fun. Remember Gary and Candi from the beginning of this chapter?

Marital Money Management– How Do We Do This?

Celebrate your victories.

It might not be time for a cruise—yet— but think of creative and affordable ways to commemorate the milestones of your financial journey. Brag on each other. Bring your kids into the loop. The two of you are working together to win with your finances, your marriage, and your life. Congratulations!

Leaving a Legacy

Proverbs 13:22 tells us that a good man leaves an inheritance for his children's children. Why, I wonder, does this inheritance include multiple generations? Children, I understand. But children's children? Could it be that this inheritance is about more than money? Perhaps this good man is to leave a legacy— one of wisdom and generosity—that will change his family tree.

Such a legacy, unlike a typical inheritance, could be passed along while the estate owner is still alive. We have friends, for example, whose son saved his pizza delivery money to spend on vacation but instead gave it all away to a homeless family. Their daughter quietly paid the mission trip fees for a man in their church. These proud parents are leaving a legacy here and now, one that will surely be passed on to their grandchildren and great grandchildren.

We close this chapter and this book with a simple question: What legacy are you leaving?

You can't change the past, but you can change the future.

Starting today.

(1) http://psychcentral.com/news/2013/07/13/money-arguments-are-top-predictor-of-divorce/57147.html

Action Items

Read 1 Corinthians 13:4–6 aloud with your spouse.
Discuss how these verses challenge you to demonstrate
more love toward each other.

Discussion Questions

How well do you and your spouse communicate about money? In what ways do you need to improve?

How can you use your differences to make your marriage stronger?

Which marital financial goals do you and your spouse need to work on?

Do the two of you agree to and live according to a budget? If not, why not?

What financial habits do you need to change so you can better influence your children?

How generous are you? What kind of giving comes easy?
Where do you struggle with giving?

How are you doing at teaching your children about money management?
What do you need to work on?

What legacy do you want to leave for your children and their children?
How are you doing?

Notes

Notes

Notes

Notes

Notes

Notes

Made in United States
Orlando, FL
05 September 2024

51173217R00057